thank you

FOR ALL YOU DO